YELLOW

My First Colors
YELLOW
AND YOU

by Candace Whitman

ABBEVILLE KIDS
A Division of Abbeville Publishing Group
New York London Paris

What can you do with yellow?

Can you make a sun?

Or a *slicker?*

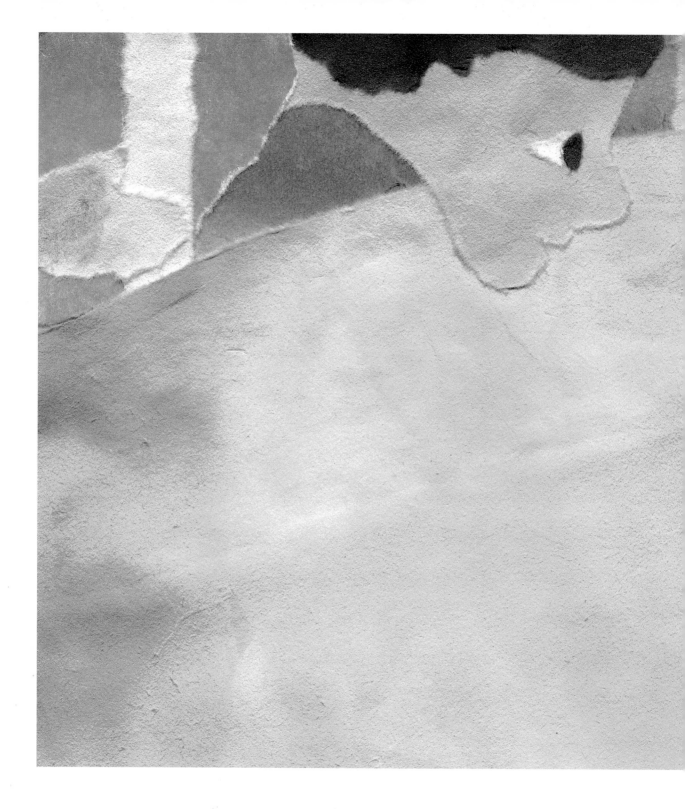

Or a blanket

for a newborn babe?

Can you make a bus?
Or a giraffe?

Or lemons for a glass of lemonade?

A little yellow fills your lap with
Pretty brown-eyed Susans,

And wraps around some juicy pears

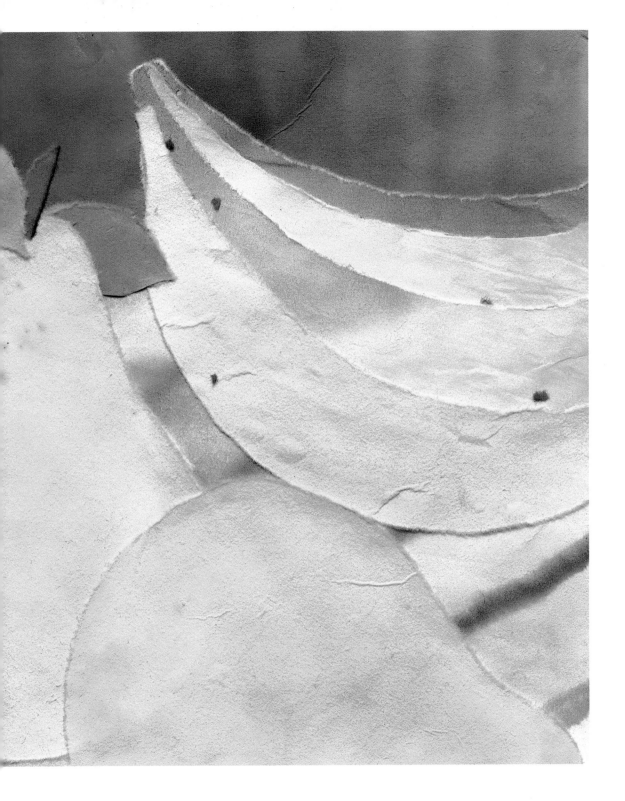

And slips down ripe bananas.

And where can you take yellow?

Do you know where it can go?

Can it ride upon the lines
Upon an open road?

Can it dot a field with lions?

Or travel on a taxi?

Will yellow be the lovely light
That glows in windows in the night?

Can yellow make your cheese Swiss cheese?

Change your bugs to bees?

Can yellow make that book
the book beside your telephone?

(Yellow's on the sticky slip of paper
with a note when you come home.)

What can you do with yellow?

Much is made
with yellow's touch—
much.

For Michaelah

Editors: Leslie Bockol and Meredith Wolf
Designer: Jordana Abrams
Production Manager: Lou Bilka

First edition
2 4 6 8 10 9 7 5 3 1

Library of Congress Cataloging-in-Publication Data
Whitman, Candace, date.
Yellow and you / by Candace Whitman. — 1st ed.
p. cm. — (My first colors)
Summary: Points out how the color yellow can be found all around us, in clothing, food, and lights in windows.
ISBN 0-7892-0308-1
1. Color—Juvenile literature. 2. Yellow—Juvenile literature.
[1. Yellow. 2. Color.] I. Title. II. Series: Whitman, Candace, date.
My first colors.
QC495.5.W52 1998
535.6—dc21 97-37819